PRAISE FOR **SMAL**

MW00414122

"A casual reunion of three longtime buddies slouching unprofitably through their 30s ultimately betrays a darker purpose in *Small Engine Repair*, a raw, funny and well-tooled new play written by and featuring John Pollono, who is making an impressive, double-barreled Off-Broadway debut."

—**Charles Isherwood**, *The New York Times*

"In a sequence of horrific, grotesque and comic twists . . . every passing remark becomes significant. A stunning investigation of classism, sexism, the lonely joys and terrors of bringing up a child, and the limits and possibilities of friendship."

—**Margaret Gray**, *Los Angeles Times*

"Once it starts humming the smart design of its engineering is clear. This is not just a profanely funny look at lugs behaving badly. It touches astutely on questions of technology, friendship, and accountability, even as it builds to a climax that takes male bonding to discomfiting extremes." —**Adam Feldman**, *TimeOut NY*

"Tawdry, nasty and fun. It's proud pulp fiction, something we don't get enough of at the theatre . . . an outrageous knockout."

—**Elisabeth Vincentelli**, *New York Post*

"An exquisitely modulated gem of a play, gripping the viewer with a storyline that is both shocking and sobering in its commentary on modern interactions in the technological age."

—**Pauline Adamek**, *LA Weekly*

"Pollono's engrossing play explores intriguing moral issues, including timely ruminations on the ill effects of the cyber age."

—**Les Spindle**, *Backstage*

"An atmospheric exploration of friendship and retribution in the wilds of Manchester, NH . . . gripping and fast-moving . . ."

—**Bob Verini**, *Variety*

JOHN POLLONO is a writer and actor who was raised in New Hampshire. He currently lives in Los Angeles with his wife and daughter.

SMALL ENGINE REPAIR

SMALL ENGINE REPAIR

A PLAY BY

JOHN POLLONO

OVERLOOK DUCKWORTH
NEW YORK • LONDON

First published in the United States and the United Kingdom in 2015 by
Overlook Duckworth, Peter Mayer Publishers, Inc.

NEW YORK
141 Wooster Street
New York, NY 10012
www.overlookpress.com
For bulk and special sales, please contact sales@overlookny.com,
or write us at the above address.

LONDON
30 Calvin Street
London E1 6NW
info@duckworth-publishers.co.uk
www.ducknet.co.uk
For bulk and special sales, please contact sales@duckworth-publishers.co.uk,
or write us at the above address.

Cataloging-in-Publication Data is available from the Library of Congress.
A catalogue record for this book is available from the British Library.

Book design and type formatting by Bernard Schleifer
Manufactured in the United States of America
ISBN 978-1-4683-0951-5 US
ISBN 978-0-7156-4961-9 UK
2 4 6 8 10 9 7 5 3 1

To Sophie Pollono

PREFACE

In 2010, I was in a play I wrote called *Lost and Found,*
which ran in the FringeNYC Festival. A bunch of buddies
I went to school with in New Hampshire came down to see
the play. Afterward we got a few beers, and they met the
actors and asked questions like "You say the same shit
every night?" and "Was that a real sandwich you made?"
and "You get to eat the sandwich after the show?" and
"What kind of sandwich was it?" As the night progressed, my
buddies hit that level of intoxication that you might see
in Manchester, NH, or even Boston but seems out of place
in Manhattan. That kind of rowdy, no-holds-barred shit where
your friend disappears and you see him two days
later sleeping in your back yard. They don't really do that
in Downtown NYC but, since they were there to see me
(and their first play ever), I felt an obligation to roll with it.

So I stopped fights, found wallets dropped in the
women's room toilet, convinced bouncers to stop the choke-
hold, asked young women not to call the cops because a
drunk guy with a thick New England accent was checking
their IDs at the door. I spent the night playing interference
and keeping the guys from getting killed or arrested. And

this thought popped in my head: *What would my life have been if I had never moved away?*

That was the WHAT IF behind *Small Engine Repair*.

The second element was the words "cock" and "cunt."

My wife runs the Late Night series (called Off-the-Clock) at our theater company, Rogue Machine Theatre. The way Late Night works is that you are given a modest budget and you have to share the set and light schematic with the "prime time" show . . . meaning you work around whatever they got. So the second those actors walk off and the final audience member vacates, you run out there and set up your show and change into your costume. Their show ends at 10 PM, yours starts at 10:30 PM. It's crazy but the good news is that you can really say and do whatever the fuck you want on stage. Experiment . . . push boundaries . . . because the folks who come out for theater at 10:30 PM tend to be more adventurous and usually a little buzzed. With this in mind, I was able to allow Packie and Swaino and Frank and Chad to talk and behave like they would if they were real people. Because it was Late Night, I didn't have to worry about offending anybody. They could be as real, misogynistic, homophobic, and idiotic as they need be.

The third element was my daughter. I did not know true joy and terror and anger until she was born. She is like Tabasco Sauce on my creativity . . . just ignites the emotions. She is jet fuel.

Needless to say, after our single preview to about six people, Jon, Mike, Josh, and I (the original cast) were pretty nervous that we were gonna get booed off the stage on opening night—particularly by female and gay theater-goers. But a strange thing happened. The vast majority of people—even respectable people—"got" the play. They understood that the play wasn't condoning or condemning the characters . . . but rather presenting them honestly, warts and all.

What made me happiest was that women loved the play the most. They saw that despite the graphic, misogynistic language and situations, testosterone, and dick jokes . . . the play is a feminist story. It just doesn't feature any women.

Nothing makes me happier than getting the approval of strong, smart women.

John Pollono
December 2014

SMALL ENGINE REPAIR

Small Engine Repair was originally produced in the United States by Jon Bernthal, Eric Bernthal, and Story Factory, LLC.

Small Engine Repair had its world premiere at Rogue Machine Theatre. Directed by Andrew Block.

FRANK	John Pollono
PACKIE	Michael Redfield
SWAINO	Jon Bernthal
CHAD	Josh Helman

Small Engine Repair had its New York premiere at the Lucille Lortel Theatre on November 18, 2013, produced by Jon Bernthal, Eric Bernthal and Story Factory, LLC, with MCC Theater.
Artistic Directors: Robert LuPone, Bernard Telsey & William Cantler.
Executive Director: Blake West.
Directed by Jo Bonney.

FRANK	John Pollono
PACKIE	James Ransone
SWAINO	James Badge Dale
CHAD	Keegan Allen

Manch-Vegas - *n - Alternative name for the city of Manchester, New Hampshire, USA. The word was coined by combining the first part of "Manchester" with the second word in "Las Vegas," juxtaposing Las Vegas's glitz and glamour with Manchester's lack of either. Used derisively.* (Urban Dictionary)

Manchester, NH. August. Present day.

A small shop. A sign for the place is prominently displayed featuring a cute, smiling six-year-old girl with a bandana around her hair, grease on her cheeks, holding a crescent wrench, and the words "Frank's Small Engine Repair, est. 1998" beneath it. There's a counter for customers to place orders for repair, set up landscaping accounts and a table with chairs for waiting.

Posters of various landscaping equipment (John Deere Tractors, etc.) decorate the wall. There is a register and some random equipment (lawnmower blades, belts, work gloves, etc.) hanging. Engines scattered about, a riding mower in a state of disrepair. There's a beatup old refrigerator somewhere, stocked with simple American beer. A door in back for the bathroom and a door in front is the main entrance. Behind the counter, beneath the main sign, is a FOURSQUARE sign.

Ted Stephens III, The Numad Group

Lights come up on FRANK ROMANOWSKI, *a solid guy in his mid/
late thirties, in the process of cleaning the place up: sweep-
ing, organizing, checking his phone and texting, occasionally
walking offstage and back on. At one point, he comes back
with a duffel bag and tucks it away somewhere. Another point
he brings on a couple paper bags containing booze.*

*He checks his phone and texts and is interrupted by a knock
on the door.* FRANK *unlocks the door with a heavy bolt (which
he relocks everytime after someone enters . . . the lock is bulky
and temperamental and requires a bit of finesse to open and
shut, although* FRANK *does it with ease) opens it to see* PACKIE
HANRAHAN, *a very small guy of the same age, who is disheveled
and dressed in grungy clothes.* PACKIE *blows right by him and
grabs a beer.*

*IMPORTANT NOTE: The characters in this play should almost
never stop drinking.*

PACKIE   Okay, just . . . let it out. Is it in your brain? Your lungs?
Your prostate? You look pale, Frank. Maybe you should sit
down. Unless it's your prostate. Then you should stand. Holy
shit, it's your fucking prostate, isn't it? Oh, man. I had a feeling.
Okay. What stage is it? Does it hurt? Does your dick still work?

FRANK   Packie. I don't have cancer.

PACKIE   You don't have cancer?

FRANK   No.

MCC/Lortel   Photo: Joan Marcus

PACKIE Does anybody in Manchester have cancer?

FRANK Nobody has cancer.

PACKIE Nobody has cancer? This is fucking infuriating. You texted me that you have cancer and I dropped everything to meet you during this crisis!

FRANK You're mad at me for not having cancer?

PACKIE Well, no . . .

FRANK And what exactly did you drop? The fucking remote control?

PACKIE I was watching the Sox in HD. I made guacamole. It's gonna spoil.

FRANK Here's your fucking guacamole.

(FRANK *tosses a five dollar bill at him.* PACKIE *stares at it.* frank *drops another two bucks and* PACKIE *takes it.*)

PACKIE (*Muttering.*) Somebody in Manch-Vegas has to have cancer. Unless they found a cure for cancer. You think I would've heard about it. I watch a lot of news . . .

FRANK Who are you talking to?

PACKIE Myself. God. I don't know. You lied to me about having cancer.

FRANK Stop fixating.

PACKIE Okay. What was so important that you'd betray our friendship?

FRANK I had to say something to get you over here because . . .

PACKIE's *phone DINGS.*

PACKIE Fuck! Toronto just scored.

FRANK Can you stop playing with your phone for five fucking seconds? Okay, look. You gotta promise me that you're not gonna freak out.

PACKIE About what?

FRANK This is me asking.

PACKIE I know it's you. You don't gotta tell me who it is. I see you right fucking there.

FRANK Swaino's coming.

PACKIE Here?

FRANK No, he's going to the Stop and Shop two towns over to buy a fucking sandwich, figured I'd mention it.

PACKIE I told you I never wanted to see him again.

FRANK Well never ends tonight.

PACKIE Jesus, Frank. This is worse than cancer. I don't wanna—

FRANK *pulls a bottle of Jameson out of a paper sack and jams it into* PACKIE's *hands.*

FRANK Pour us a shot of that Jameson, will ya?

PACKIE I thought you stopped drinking?

FRANK Just fucking pour.

PACKIE I cut back too, Frank. For health reasons.

FRANK Really? Because a month ago I got a call, carried you out of Smudgie's Pub and brought you home, you were so hammered you had shit your pants.

PACKIE   That's why I woke up in the tub.

Knock at the door.

FRANK   If he starts something I'll deal with it, okay?

PACKIE   I don't need you defending me.

FRANK   I'm just saying.

PACKIE   Just get the fucking door.

FRANK *opens the door to find a man in his thirties,* TERENCE SWAINO. SWAINO *is dressed in what he perceives to be very trendy clothes.*

FRANK   Swaino.

SWAINO   Whatsup, guy? (*They hug.*) Damn, you're like a piece of rock. What's got you so tense?

FRANK   Work. How you been?

SWAINO   Got blown an hour ago.

SWAINO *takes a few steps inside and pauses as he sees* PACKIE. *After a moment, he breaks the tension:*

SWAINO   When'd you get a Chihuahua?

PACKIE   Hardy har.

SWAINO   I always pegged you as a Pit Bull man, Frank. I'm surprised you'd spend money on a designer Mexican toy breed.

PACKIE   If I'm a Chihuahua then you're a fucking Corgi.

SWAINO   That's not a burn, Packie. You gotta one-up me with a smaller dog.

PACKIE   Corgi is a smaller dog.

SWAINO   Corgi is practically a regular sized dog. They just got wicked short legs. You shoulda said Yorkshire Terrier.

PACKIE   Well that breed isn't smaller than a Chihuahua. I know, my Grammy had one.

SWAINO   That was a Maltese. And it was a mix.

PACKIE   It was not!

SWAINO   It had white fucking fur and—Jesus, Packie. Trading barbs with you is like throwing rocks at a retard.

PACKIE   Hey! You know my Uncle Gary has Down's Syndrome!

SWAINO   Sorry. Trading barbs with you is like throwing rocks at Uncle Gary.

FRANK   Knock it off, Swaino. You two even remember what you were fighting about anymore?

PACKIE   Fucking cough drops.

SWAINO   You shouldn't have grabbed those cough drops outta my fucking hand, Packie.

PACKIE   I had a sore throat.

SWAINO   I told you to get your own!

PACKIE   You were talking to some chick and wanted to look cool, as usual, so you insulted me.

SWAINO   I called you a leprechaun! Big fucking deal!

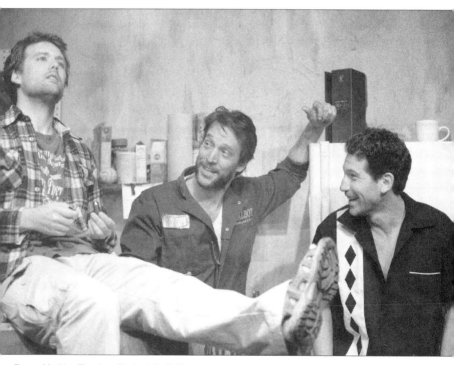

Rogue Machine Theatre   Photo: John P. Flynn

PACKIE As an Irish American, I find that offensive!

SWAINO I'm half fucking Irish.

PACKIE Exactly. You're a traitor.

SWAINO And you're magically delicious.

> PACKIE *lunges at* SWAINO. FRANK *stops him.*

FRANK Hey! Knock it off.

SWAINO What?

FRANK Packie?

PACKIE What do you want me to say?

> FRANK *pours them each a shot as he lets them have it.*

FRANK Listen to me. You guys can't let thirty plus years of history
get flushed down the toilet over fucking cough drops. Okay?
Now I was there and I was sober and I saw the whole fucking
thing. Packie, you were a little out of control that night and you
acted like an ass. You fixated on those cough drops—

PACKIE But, Frank—

FRANK You fixated on those cough drops like you sometimes
fixate on things when you've been drinking and you should have
let Swaino talk to that girl.

SWAINO Yeah.

FRANK And you, there was no acceptable reason for you to
pound on Packie like that. He was too hammered to defend
himself. You shoulda waited until the next day when he could
have at least fought back a little. He had to get stitches.

MCC/Lortel   Photo: Joan Marcus

SWAINO Frank, I—

FRANK Who do you think got to pay for that fucking situation? You know this guy doesn't have goddamn insurance.

PACKIE I don't.

FRANK *hands them the shots. He pours one for himself and lifts it up.*

FRANK To friends. May we always be there for one another in our time of need.

They drink.

SWAINO So when are the strippers coming?

PACKIE What strippers?

SWAINO The fucking . . . I don't know, the fucking strippers. Frank said come by because he's ordering strippers.

PACKIE If you were a real friend you'd know that Frank's against strippers on account of him having a daughter of stripper age.

SWAINO Am I speaking American here? He ordered strippers. Maybe if you were a real friend you'd see that Frank had a change of heart and didn't want you judging him.

PACKIE You motherfucker. You shift your moral compass in regards to strippers and I don't know about it?

FRANK There's no strippers coming.

SWAINO I got twenty fucking dollars in singles here.

FRANK You wouldn't return my texts. I hadda make something up to get you here.

MCC/Lortel   Photo: Joan Marcus

SWAINO This is bullshit. I had plans tonight with some friends.

FRANK We're not friends?

SWAINO Adult friends. Not childhood friends.

PACKIE We're adults.

SWAINO You're almost thirty-six years old, Packie. That's like nursery school age in leprechaun years.

PACKIE I know you can kick my ass but I swear to God I'll break a coupla your fingers first.

FRANK Packie, relax.

PACKIE I told you I didn't wanna see this guy.

SWAINO You got no reason to be pissed at me, Packie. I don't got your pot of gold.

PACKIE You know how I am! And you play games!

FRANK He's just fucking around, Packie!

PACKIE I gotta take a piss.

PACKIE *walks out.*

FRANK What's wrong with you?

SWAINO The material just, like, flows out of me. I can't help it.

FRANK He's one of your best friends.

SWAINO Fifteen years ago, maybe. Why all the fucking lying to get us to hang out?

FRANK It's been too long we all got together.

SWAINO Yeah, maybe there's a reason.

SWAINO *takes out a tube of hand lotion and applies it.*

FRANK   What the fuck is that?

SWAINO   Moisturizer.

FRANK   Since when?

SWAINO   You didn't get the certified letter I sent you last April saying I was gonna start using moisturizer?

FRANK   It smells like fucking ice cream.

SWAINO   It's vanilla. Go ahead, mock me. But take a look at your fucking hands, Frank. Working with grease and shit all day. They're disgusting. You think chicks wanna be pawed over with greasy fucking zombie hands?

FRANK   Listen, Packie still lives in his grandmother's basement and hasn't worked a steady job in two years. Give him a fucking break.

SWAINO   What do you want me to say? I look at him, I just see a fucking burnout who needs somebody to snap him out of it.

FRANK   So it's your job to mock him into leading a productive life? He looks up to you.

SWAINO   When you start drinking again?

FRANK   How's that thing?

SWAINO   Not panning out. Why?

FRANK   Just wondering.

SWAINO   I'm gonna pay you back.

FRANK   I'm not worried about that.

SWAINO   So why you fucking bring it up?

FRANK   Because we're friends and I was fucking inquiring about your life. Jesus Christ. You know what? Fuck it. Go be with your adult friends.

SWAINO   Aw, Frank. Did I hurt yer feelings? I'm wicked sorry.

PACKIE *comes out zipping up his fly. Sees them looking at him.*

PACKIE   Despite what you assholes think, I have feelings. I come from a long line of proud Irish immigrants and I will not stand here and listen to you mock my heritage. My people have been oppressed by white men for too long to put up with . . . stop laughing, I mean it. You know . . . fuck you guys.

FRANK   Relax, Packie.

FRANK *opens a beer and hands it to him.*

SWAINO   Drink up.

PACKIE   You guys eating ice cream?

SWAINO   Don't fucking push me, Packie.

PACKIE   What did I do?

FRANK   Everybody just calm down for a second, okay? Got a little surprise for you pussies.

FRANK *pulls a bottle (that comes in a display box) of Johnny Walker Blue.*

PACKIE   Johnny Walker Blue?

SWAINO   Jesus Christ, Frank. This is like two hundred bucks.

FRANK   Want to make sure tonight is special.

SWAINO   I'll admit, the night went from sucks shit to just sucks ass.

He fills their glasses and they drink, taking a moment to enjoy.

PACKIE   Tastes like the tears of angels, Frank.

FRANK   How's the job hunt, Packie?

PACKIE   It's a depressed economy. What are you gonna do? Swaino, they hiring at the warehouse?

SWAINO   You get in the union?

PACKIE   No.

SWAINO   Then ya just answered your own fucking question.

PACKIE   Okay, so how do I get in the union?

SWAINO   Get a union job.

PACKIE   But you just said they won't hire me unless I'm in the union.

SWAINO   I hear ya. It's a fucking conundrum.

PACKIE   You don't even know what the fuck a conundrum is!

SWAINO   Yeah I do.

PACKIE   Prove it. What's it mean?

SWAINO   Means . . . you ain't getting a job, Packie. That's what it means.

PACKIE   Frank! I'm so fucking frustrated right now!

FRANK All right, all right. Let's choose another fucking topic here.

SWAINO How's Grammy Hanrahan these days?

PACKIE Still drinks whiskey every morning. Still smells like Peppermint Patties.

SWAINO How the fuck old is she now?

PACKIE Ninety-one, can you believe it?

SWAINO Remember that time, in like third grade, when we all saw her bush?

PACKIE Why you gotta always bring that up?

FRANK How do you not bring that up?

SWAINO She's making breakfast, turns around and, whaddya know, no pants!

FRANK First real bush I ever saw.

SWAINO Looked like a baby gray squirrel.

PACKIE Leave her alone.

SWAINO She still drive that '76 Monte Carlo?

PACKIE God no. Sold it after she ran over that postal worker. I drive her if she needs to go someplace. But she's ninety-one, where the fuck's she gonna go?

SWAINO I got a funny story. Remember that chick I introduced to you guys at Frank's barbecue a few summers ago? Twenty-three-year-old from Pelham?

PACKIE Pakistani gal?

SWAINO Yeah.

PACKIE Her name was Afnahn.

SWAINO How do you remember her fucking name?

PACKIE We had a great discussion about Islamic values.

SWAINO Anyway, we kinda lost touch after I stopped calling her and then, a few weeks ago, I'm at the Black Brimmer with some friends, I see her making eyes at me across the way. So I go over, we start chatting and she's pretending she doesn't remember me, right? She gives me a fake name, so I give her a fake name. Then I realize she's playing like a sex game. So I go along and to be honest, it's kinda turning me on. I give her a whole fake backstory that I'm from fucking Connecticut and shit and she's eating it up. We're having fun, going with it. We go back to my place, hosed at this point. We fuck for a while, she comes a second time, I pass out. Wake up the next day and she's laying there in the morning light and it finally fucking dawns on me . . .

PACKIE It's a different girl.

SWAINO How did you know that?

PACKIE I'm right?

SWAINO What?

FRANK What?

SWAINO G'head, Frank.

FRANK What?

SWAINO Let's hear it.

FRANK What?

SWAINO The fucking speech.

FRANK What fucking speech?

SWAINO The fucking speech about how I'll never meet a quality chick, I should settle down, blah fucking blah.

FRANK Sounds like you got it covered.

SWAINO My other friends thought that story was fucking hilarious.

FRANK *fills up* SWAINO*'s drink.*

FRANK When we were young did we ever think we'd be sharing a whole bottle of Johnny Blue?

PACKIE I set my dreams a little higher, Frank.

FRANK Of course you did.

SWAINO So how's Crystal these days?

FRANK Good.

SWAINO She's what? Seventeen now?

FRANK Yeah.

SWAINO Feel like I haven't seen her since you guys moved to Derry.

FRANK *shows* SWAINO *and* PACKIE *a picture from his phone.*

FRANK I took this picture a coupla months ago . . .

SWAINO Barely recognize her. She's like an adult now.

PACKIE She's beautiful, Frank.

PACKIE *walks over to the sign in the back.*

PACKIE I remember the day Swaino took that picture of her. Sunday afternoon and we were barbequing out back for her birthday. You gave her that John Deere riding lawnmower you fixed up and pulled the blades outta, painted it pink.

SWAINO Frank, you couldn't get her offa that thing.

FRANK I thought she'd get tired after the second tank of gas.

PACKIE She'd charge me fifty cents to drive from one end of the parking lot, where we was barbequing, to the other where we kept the cooler. Fifty cents! But I paid her. Back then I had money.

SWAINO After what? Three fucking hours thing snapped a belt?

PACKIE Then Crystal grabs that crescent wrench and says she's gonna fix it just like Daddy. Wicked cute moment.

SWAINO I whipped out my camera and captured Frank's Small Engine Repair's definitive fucking image. You know, I should get residuals.

FRANK You're drinking your residuals.

SWAINO What ever happened to the pink John Deere?

FRANK Keep it in the garage under a tarp.

PACKIE Seems like just, like, months ago. But it was ten fucking years. Weird thinking about that . . . time moves so much different for you when you're a kid, don't it? Makes me feel really fucking old.

SWAINO We're not that old.

PACKIE Sure we are.

SWAINO Until we cross forty, we're still considered young by culture.

PACKIE Dude, we're middle age.

FRANK We're not middle age.

PACKIE You're thirty-six, right?

FRANK Something like that.

PACKIE How old was your dad when he died?

FRANK Fuck you.

SWAINO My secret to youth? Don't date 'em over twenty-six. Older than that . . . their pussies reek of death.

FRANK Women don't know how to make love until they're thirty.

SWAINO I prefer a girl who doesn't know how to fuck.

FRANK So she won't be disappointed?

SWAINO No, asshole. I want a clean slate.

PACKIE A clean sheet?

SWAINO Slate dipshit. Truth is that most girls have had bad sexual experiences and they bring those issues in bed, gets all complicated. I'd rather be there in the beginning before all that shit happens.

FRANK You wanna be the bad experience.

SWAINO Pretty much.

PACKIE Crystal going to college?

FRANK That's the plan.

SWAINO Who knew that orgasm your junior year would go to fucking college.

PACKIE Not to get too deep, but if you woulda pulled out that night your whole life woulda been different.

FRANK She's the best thing that ever happened to me.

SWAINO We know. She's a blessing. It's just crazy thinking about it . . . one ill-timed cumshot can alter the trajectory of your whole fucking life.

PACKIE Crystal going to college is a crazy accomplishment. I just mean, you was eighteen and took on practically all that responsibility by yourself. Statistically speaking, in a lot of those situations, girl ends up being a stripper . . .

FRANK You fucking cocksucker—!

SWAINO Whoa, whoa. You think this tight ass would ever let that happen?

PACKIE None of us would.

SWAINO Right, with Uncle Packie as a role model it's surprising she's not running for Congress.

PACKIE I helped out a lot back in the day.

SWAINO You ever change a diaper, douche bag?

PACKIE Have you?

SWAINO Only a thousand. My sisters had babies coming out of their asses growing up. I was changing diapers when I was fucking nine years old. I love babies. Everybody knows this about me.

PACKIE Frank?

FRANK You did shit too, Packie. You both did. I couldn't have done it without you two.

SWAINO So what colleges she applying to?

FRANK A bunch.

SWAINO "A bunch?" What the fuck?

FRANK What?

SWAINO Usually we start talking about her you don't fucking stop. You're all like "Crystal wrote this poem on Theodore Roosevelt, made me fucking cry . . ." Faggy dad shit like that.

FRANK I'm just enjoying the fucking Scotch.

PACKIE She should get a degree in marketing or technology or something.

SWAINO What the fuck do you know about it?

PACKIE I'm up to date on all the current trends. You see that sign over there? Frank paid me to set that up.

SWAINO What the fuck is Foursquare?

FRANK I still don't know what the fuck that means.

PACKIE Customers come in, they activate Foursquare and it posts on their various social networks that they've been here.

SWAINO So?

PACKIE What do you mean?

SWAINO I mean, why do we give a fuck where some other asshole's been?

PACKIE It's called Social Networking.

SWAINO My balls have social networking.

PACKIE Fuck you, I bet you don't even have internet on your phone.

SWAINO Yeah? Look at this. That's the motherfucking Blackberry Storm, bitch. It's got internet and all that bullshit. I get fucking email. Weather.

PACKIE They don't even make this anymore.

SWAINO What are you, an Asian teenager?

PACKIE How many friends you got on Facebook?

SWAINO How much can you bench press?

PACKIE Frank benches more than you.

SWAINO You're such a twat.

FRANK Less talking, more drinking.

They each do a shot in unison.

PACKIE Hey Frank, I've been meaning to tell you something. Now don't over react, but I saw somebody recently.

FRANK Who?

PACKIE Karen Delgado.

SWAINO What's the matter with you, bringing that up?

PACKIE Did you know she's back?

FRANK She's the mother of my child, you don't think I'd know she's back in Manch-Vegas?

SWAINO So you've seen her?

FRANK She got in town three days ago, staying at her aunt's. I met her for lunch.

SWAINO The fucking cycle begins.

FRANK We had fucking roast beef sandwiches. She doesn't even have our new address.

SWAINO That cunt doesn't deserve roast beef.

FRANK Look, I'm serious. She's the mother of my child. You can call her a bitch but not a cunt.

SWAINO Sorry, but she is the definition of the word.

PACKIE Enough, man.

SWAINO Look it up in the dictionary. C – U – N – T.

PACKIE Swaino—

SWAINO What, I can't even spell it?

FRANK Enough!

SWAINO You want us to pretend we're happy she's back? So we can deal with your anger issues again?

FRANK You don't have to deal with shit anymore, Swaino. I see you what? Twice a year now?

SWAINO Whether or not the three of us are chums anymore ain't the goddamn point. Karen is fucking toxic. She comes around whenever the she wants to, plays the mother, the wife for a few weeks. Pulls you in. Then tears it all up, you go on a bender and start throwing strangers she flirts with through plate glass fucking windows. I stay up all night with Crystal, telling her her father ain't going to jail.

FRANK I'm not like that anymore.

SWAINO I see, you're Mr. Even Temper now. Because you've got that fantastic look in your eye.

PACKIE Swaino, shut the fuck up.

FRANK Why don't you aim that brilliant insight in your own direction, Swaino?

SWAINO Fuck you and your high horse.

FRANK At least I accept responsibility. Raising a kid instead of spending five hundred bucks on car speakers.

SWAINO Those are great fucking speakers.

FRANK G'head, laugh it off. But so you know, this shaggy I-don't-give-a-fuck routine you started in junior high is getting kinda sad. Terence Swaino being too super cool for Geometry was pretty fucking awesome, I'll admit it. But now? Maybe you oughta think about what you wanna be when you grow up.

PACKIE Relax, Frank.

FRANK This is my place, I say when I relax.

SWAINO Hope you don't act this way in front of Crystal. Teenagers are very impressionable.

FRANK *picks up a basketball and hurls it across the room, where it crashes into a shelf.*

FRANK I guess sticking that diseased cock of yours in a buncha half dumb girls make you a tough guy alla sudden. Go ahead, take a fucking swing, Terence. Take the first shot, see what happens when you do. See what happens. I'm kinda curious.

SWAINO   I gotta take a piss.

SWAINO *walks out.*

PACKIE   What's a matter with you?

FRANK   Every coupla years he pulls this shit . . .

PACKIE   Frank, don't be so hard on him. In his own idiotic way he's trying to help.

FRANK   He's a self-serving prick.

PACKIE   And this is news? Come on. You got everything. What's he got?

FRANK   This coming from you?

PACKIE   I'm not the one who dragged us here under false pretenses.

FRANK   I just wanted us together again, like the old days. What the fuck's wrong with that?

PACKIE   Honestly? These days I prefer spending time alone.

FRANK   That's pathetic.

PACKIE   Maybe Swaino likes these new friends because he's been able to establish a new position in their group. He's not the middle man no more. He's the Frank.

FRANK   You make it seem like we got a choice. Thirty years, we're practically family.

PACKIE   But we're not. Have another drink, Frank. You always got a lot on your mind. Let's not think about anything tonight.

SWAINO *comes back in.* FRANK *carries over a fresh beer.*

FRANK   Hey.

SWAINO   Hey.

FRANK   I'm sorry I called your cock diseased. (*To* SWAINO*'s cock.*) I'm sorry.

FRANK *opens the beer for* SWAINO*'s cock. Then hands it to* SWAINO*.*

SWAINO   I took a needle for that situation. So if you're gonna make fun of my cock, you shall henceforth refer to it as a "formerly diseased" cock.

FRANK   So a few months ago, I'm dating this woman. Second date. She's thirty-two, divorced. Got a four-year-old son . . .

SWAINO   This is fucking depressing.

FRANK   She had wicked big tits.

SWAINO   All right, I'm intrigued. Go on.

FRANK   We end up at her place. She puts the kid to sleep and we start fooling around in her bed. And she's, like, a madwoman. Tells me she hasn't been with a guy since her kid's born. So I peel off her jeans and she says "Aw shit . . ." I look down and she's got this huge, unkempt, like, 1970s bush. It's like a fucking Hell's Angel beard. She says "I'm wicked embarrassed, Frank. I was gonna trim but my kid got sick and I forgot." She's a single mom, when the fuck she have time? So we both start cracking up. Her kid wakes up starts crying. So she throws her clothes back on and says "don't go anywhere, Frank, I'll be right back." I'm lying there in her bed—naked—

for like an hour . . . my hard-on is a distant fucking memory at this point. I get dressed, peek into the room and I see her lying there on this, like, racecar bed . . . spooning her son . . . both snoring. So I watch for a coupla minutes. It's kind of a sweet image, you know. A mother like that with her kid like that. I let myself out, go home and watch TV.

SWAINO You ever consider killing yourself?

PACKIE You ever see her again?

FRANK She never called.

SWAINO You know why? She was insulted. Before you left, you should have jerked off on her pillow. At least then she woulda known you were attracted to her.

FRANK Good point. I shoulda thought of that.

SWAINO Hey, man. You ever want to read a page from the Book of Swaino, I'm here for you.

They tap glasses.

PACKIE Yeah . . . it's too bad you never fell in love after Karen.

FRANK I gotta take a piss.

FRANK *walks out and slams the door behind him.*

SWAINO What's a matter with you?

PACKIE What?

SWAINO You think he's happy that Crystal grew up with virtually no consistent fucking females around? Not cool.

PACKIE I didn't think about that.

SWAINO The shit you don't fucking think about could fill Fenway, Packie.

PACKIE I'm such an asshole.

SWAINO I've been trying to tell you that for years.

PACKIE He hates me.

SWAINO Nobody takes the shit you say seriously anyway. Just . . . think next time. So tell me about this Foursquare bullshit. I gotta be hip on all the shit my female demographic is into.

PACKIE Okay, gimme your phone.

Hands it to him.

PACKIE Okay, you open your Facebook app. Where's your Facebook app? You don't have many apps on your phone.

SWAINO Say "app" one more fucking time.

PACKIE It's an application.

SWAINO Well just fucking say that. How much time you really save abbreviating the word?

PACKIE That's what it's called, I don't know.

SWAINO I just go on the internet part.

PACKIE The application is already installed, idiot. You just press this . . . then go here and press this and look—

SWAINO Look at that "Terence Swaino just checked in at Frank's Small Engine Repair on July 2 at 9: 38 P.M." Gotta admit, that's kinda sweet.

PACKIE See, I just did it too. Now the whole world knows we're here.

SWAINO   Yay. Well, you know, if it helps Frank's business . . .

PACKIE   Why won't you accept my friend request?

SWAINO   You really want me to answer that?

PACKIE   I'm gonna accept it.

SWAINO   Gimme that back.

PACKIE *presses some buttons.*

PACKIE   What is this?

SWAINO   What?

PACKIE   Karen Delgado posted on your wall "Thanks for the drinks and the advice." Yesterday.

SWAINO   It's not what you think!

PACKIE   What the fuck is this?

PACKIE *starts running around the shop, avoiding him.*

SWAINO   Gimme the fucking phone!

PACKIE   Are you banging Karen?

SWAINO   No!

PACKIE   Is she the one who blew you?

SWAINO   No, asshole. Gimme the phone.

PACKIE   You gotta tell Frank, Swaino. He's gonna go ballistic he finds out.

SWAINO   I didn't do anything. Gimme that fucking phone!

FRANK *comes in the room and they stop and try to look natural.* FRANK *is on the phone.*

FRANK   No, we're not there anymore. Just head south on Mammoth Road, take your second left. Go around back, gate's unlocked. Okay. Yeah. See you in a minute.

FRANK *walks over and pours shot and downs it.*

PACKIE   Who was that?

FRANK   This kid.

PACKIE   Kid?

FRANK   He's like twenty. Met him playing basketball, we hung out a few times, I told him to stop by.

SWAINO   Why the fuck would you do that?

FRANK   Thought you guys might find him amusing.

PACKIE   In what way?

FRANK   What's the big fucking deal?

SWAINO   Are you having sex with this kid?

FRANK   Jesus, what's the matter with you? He's just a kid from Cambridge, played pick-up basketball with him a few times at the gym down there, I figure why the fuck n—

SWAINO   What the fuck you doing in Cambridge?

FRANK   Work shit. What?

PACKIE   It's cool, Frank.

SWAINO   Yeah, it's cool. It's wicked gay, but it's cool.

FRANK   You hang out with twenty-year-olds all the time.

SWAINO   If you don't see the difference then you really must be sucking his cock.

FRANK Jerk offs.

PACKIE Frank, I'm just not in the mood to meet new people.

SWAINO If Packie's leaving, I'm not gonna be the third wheel in your psychologically disturbing assfucking.

FRANK Come on. Stop being such fucking cunts. I told him to come by because I'm buying some Ecstasy off him.

PACKIE Why didn't you just say so?

FRANK It was a surprise.

PACKIE Frank, you're full of surprises tonight. It's weird.

SWAINO Since when do you do Ex?

FRANK I don't. But I figured I could try it tonight with you guys.

SWAINO And then what? Dance with each other in your fucking lawnmower shop?

FRANK No, we can hit a club or something.

SWAINO In Manch-Vegas?

FRANK We'll get wicked fucked up, I'll pay for a cab.

SWAINO What club?

PACKIE You're the fucking expert.

SWAINO We're not dressed for it.

FRANK You two have been trying to get me to take Ex for seven fucking years. I figured I'd try it tonight. What's the big deal?

PACKIE Come on, Swaino. Don't be a pussy.

SWAINO Fine. Why the fuck not.

PACKIE *pulls out a pipe from his pocket, hops up on the counter and takes a monster hit.*

PACKIE If we're going out then I'm smoking up, anybody else?

SWAINO Sure.

FRANK Why the fuck not?

PACKIE I like this new, out-of-control Frank. Been a long time since you've let your hair down like this.

SWAINO "Let your hair down?"

PACKIE It means, like, relax.

FRANK We know what it means. But who without a vagina actually fucking says that?

PACKIE What?

They stand in silence a moment, let the weed hit.

PACKIE So last March at my cousin's bachelor party, this stripper puts her pinkie finger in my ass.

FRANK *and* SWAINO *break up laughing.*

PACKIE Are you laughing with me or at me?

This makes them laugh even more.

PACKIE I thought everyone was sharing.

There's a knock at the door. FRANK *walks toward it, pauses.*

FRANK Listen, I don't want him to know that I have a daughter.

SWAINO Afraid your drug dealer won't think you're cool?

FRANK Just do me a favor, okay?

SWAINO Are you serious?

FRANK Yes.

SWAINO You want us to laugh at everything you say too?

FRANK I'll leave that up to you.

PACKIE Should we let our hair down?

> SWAINO *and* FRANK *just stare at him.*

PACKIE Sorry . . .

> FRANK *opens the door and we see* CHAD WALKER, *ninteen, super clean cut, preppy, athletic and handsome.*

CHAD What's up, Frank?

They shake hands.

FRANK Hey, man. Thanks for coming out all this way.

CHAD It's cool. I'm meeting some Lambdas in Portsmouth tonight anyway.

FRANK Lambdas, huh? So these are my boys. Packie is the sawed-off, Chihuahua-looking burnout whose pants, you'd be surprised to know, hide a disproportionately massive cock. If you stick around, he'll probably pull it out at some point, he does that when he drinks.

PACKIE I do. Nice to meet you.

CHAD T'sup.

FRANK And this pathetic degenerate who smells like vanilla fucking ice cream is Swaino. Be careful of this one. He'll stick his dick into anything with a hole and a heartbeat.

SWAINO I'll bet your asshole feels just like your sister's pussy.

CHAD Awesome.

FRANK Guys, this is Chad Walker. He's a Mass-hole.

PACKIE Welcome to Manch-Vegas, Chad.

CHAD This is quite a majestic city you have here.

PACKIE Is he being sarcastic?

SWAINO What do you think?

FRANK You want a beer?

CHAD Sure.

FRANK Make yourself at home.

FRANK *pulls a beer outta the fridge, offers it to him. Then he stands there . . . awkwardly . . . genuinely uncomfortable.*

FRANK So. Should we, uh . . . you know . . . with the, uh..?

CHAD You mean this?

CHAD *hands him a clear baggie with pills.*

FRANK Wow. Just, like, out in the open like that?

CHAD What do you mean?

SWAINO This is Frank's first big drug deal. I think he thought there'd be code words or something.

FRANK I'll get your money.

Rogue Machine Theatre   Photo: John P. Flynn

FRANK *is about to open a drawer.*

SWAINO Wait, don't move. Packie, how much you wanna bet Frank put the money in, like, a folded-up brown manila envelope.

PACKIE Or how about a roll of cash with a rubber band on it?

SWAINO I'm going with envelope. Okay, Frank. Go ahead.

FRANK Fuck you guys.

FRANK *pulls out a folded up brown manila envelope.* SWAINO *celebrates his victory.*

FRANK I'm sorry that I'm not a professional drug buyer like you two fucking twats.

CHAD Hey, I'm not a professional either, dude.

FRANK I know, man. I was fucking with them. I didn't mean to bust your balls.

CHAD I usually only sell to guys in my fraternity.

FRANK I appreciate you opening the circle for me.

CHAD You'll dig that shit. Best Molly in the city.

FRANK Who's Molly? I thought this was Ecstasy?

SWAINO It's the same fucking thing.

PACKIE How old are you, Chad?

CHAD Almost twenty.

PACKIE So that means you're less than two decades old?

CHAD Yes.

PACKIE Amazing.

CHAD I had very little to do with it.

PACKIE LOL.

SWAINO Seriously with the fucking "LOL?"

CHAD Hey, man. Give me a hit off that.

SWAINO Please. Let's unite the generations.

PACKIE What do you drive?

CHAD Bimmer.

PACKIE Nice. And how much can you bench press?

SWAINO Enough with the questions.

CHAD I don't use free weights. Makes your fast twitch muscles less responsive. I'm training with Plyometrics and Pilates now, totally improved my vertical.

SWAINO You play division one ball?

CHAD I'm on the team at Northeastern.

SWAINO I meant high school.

CHAD Yeah, we were Div one.

SWAINO Us too.

PACKIE But he played in Massachusetts. It's a whole different thing down there. They compete against black people.

CHAD Coach says I'm gonna be a starter this year, only a sophomore.

SWAINO You must get some serious pussy.

CHAD I do all right.

SWAINO Yeah?

CHAD Yeah.

SWAINO Yeah.

CHAD What are you guys drinking?

PACKIE Johnny Walker Blue.

SWAINO *looks to* FRANK*, gets the okay, pours the kid a glass of Johnny Blue.* CHAD *takes a gulp.*

CHAD That tastes like shit.

SWAINO You, my friend, are what doctors refer to as a fucking retard.

PACKIE Swaino, my uncle.

SWAINO You, my friend, are what doctors refer to as Uncle Gary.

CHAD Old dudes always drink Scotch. Why's it so important to like Scotch?

PACKIE In ten years I'm gonna ask you that question and you know what you're gonna say?

CHAD What?

PACKIE You know I started that out thinking I could come up with something wicked funny but it never, like, gelled.

SWAINO Hey, since you're from Generation-whatever-the-fuck, do you know what that sign over there means?

CHAD Foursquare? Sure.

PACKIE See?

SWAINO Packie's like a teenager in that he's wicked up to date on the current trends and also that he doesn't have a fucking job.

CHAD Sick. I just checked in.

He holds up his phone to show them.

CHAD And a friend request from Patrick Han . . .

PACKIE Hanrahan. It's Irish.

SWAINO Jesus Christ, Packie. Give the kid a fucking break.

PACKIE What? His generation is fully immersed in technology. A friend request is like a handshake.

CHAD So when you guys were my age there was, like, no internet?

FRANK Somehow we survived.

PACKIE It sucked.

SWAINO It was way better.

PACKIE How?

SWAINO We used to do this thing called going outside.

PACKIE What's so good about outside?

SWAINO Have you seen yourself lately? You look like something a Japanese fisherman snagged off the bottom of the fucking ocean with his anchor. You need to invest in sunlight.

PACKIE The internet has revolutionized the world.

SWAINO The only thing the internet revolutionized is jerking off.

FRANK Remember when we were kids, we had one playboy for three years, traded it back and forth.

MCC/Lortel   Photo: Joan Marcus

SWAINO There's your social networking, Packie.

FRANK Now, with one click, you can see a girl eating shit out of another girl's ass.

PACKIE You watched that video I sent you!

FRANK Since that video, I delete every fucking email you send me.

CHAD You talking about "Two Girls, One Cup?"

PACKIE It's amazing, right?

FRANK Explain this to me. How is that healthy to watch?

CHAD It's not healthy, it's just funny.

SWAINO Frank thinks the internet exists mainly to degrade women. He doesn't understand that guys are biologically designed to wanna fuck everything and the internet didn't invent that. Cavemen used to look at rocks that resembled big tits, jerk off all over them. True story.

PACKIE Hey. I think Frank's kinda right. Some of these amateur videos, these girls clearly have family-type issues and I feel bad for them.

SWAINO But you still yank it to them?

PACKIE By then the damage is already done.

FRANK Fucking degenerate.

SWAINO Calm down, Batman. We have guests.

FRANK *does another shot.*

SWAINO Maybe you slow down a little?

CHAD How do you guys know each other?

FRANK Swaino moved across the street from me in the first grade. Packie was born in the house behind him.

SWAINO He means literally born in the house. His parents were very odd people.

PACKIE They was just poor.

SWAINO I was, like, the bridge that united us. I had a finished basement, it was a real draw.

CHAD Where did you guys go to school?

PACKIE Central High.

CHAD I mean college.

SWAINO I did a year, Keene State.

A buzz and CHAD *looks at his iPhone.*

CHAD Sox just beat Toronto.

PACKIE What was the final score?

CHAD 4 to 1.

PACKIE See? The internet's not all evil. Can't think of the last time we went to Fenway.

SWAINO Too fucking expensive now that they win.

CHAD We have season tickets.

SWAINO See? You can go with your new friend.

CHAD I'd have been there tonight but my dad had to bring the fucking CEO of Dunkin Donuts.

PACKIE Speaking of Scotch, remember the night after Game 6?

SWAINO This fucking story again?

CHAD The Buckner game?

PACKIE Right. 1986

SWAINO Your parents were still giving each other hand jobs back then.

PACKIE Sox lead the series going in. Me and Frank and Swaino are in Swaino's basement watching this shitty little black and white with aluminum foil on the antenna. The Old Men are upstairs watching the same game on the color TV. Our fathers used to get hammered when they put money on the game and they'd get wicked fucking worked up. Slightest thing would set them off. That night it was worse. Because the Sox gave New Englanders something they hadn't had in a long time . . . Hope.

SWAINO What is this, a fucking Ken Burns documentary?

PACKIE Like you watch documentaries?

CHAD You don't need to relive it, I actually know the game pretty well.

FRANK He's not really talking to anyone specific at this point.

PACKIE Boston took a quick 2–0 lead on RBI base hits from Dwight Evans and Marty Barrett. The Mets tied in the fifth on a single from Ray Knight and a run-scoring double play by Danny Heep. An error by Knight led to Barrett scoring in the seventh to give Boston a 3–2 lead . . . Mookie Wilson is coming up for the Mets so McNamara pulls Shiraldi and puts Stanley on the mound. Mookie has the most epic at bat ever, Mitchell scores on a wild pitch. It's a full count . . . nine fucking pitches gone by and Mookie connects and it's a slow roller, bounces right up the first base line . . . Bill Buckner squares up, drops his glove and . . . the fucking ball rolls right between his goddamn legs. One of the worst errors in baseball history!

CHAD   I just pulled up the video on YouTube.

PACKIE   But that night doesn't end there for us. Right after Buckner's historic fuckup, something happens that chills our blood. Upstairs, the Old Men are dead silent. Not a good sign. So what do we do? We literally take our fucking shoes off and start tiptoeing out in our socks. Problem is, you hadda walk up the stairs to get outside and Swaino's pop spotted him. He grabs Swaino by the neck and slams him against the fridge. What does Frank do? He jumps on Swaino's pop's back and tries to get him in a headlock. Now this type of kid on adult attack was unprecedented in our world and highly ineffective since Frank is like a bony eleven-year-old. Also, let me state for the record that Swaino's pop was in Vietnam and literally killed Victor Charlie, this man can destroy people. But he doesn't hafta 'cause Frank's Old Man sees this, literally kicks Frank in the ass, knocks him off and jumps on him. So I'm standing there watching my two best friends get demolished by their fathers in the middle of the kitchen. I look beside me and there's my old man. I look at him, he looks at me, we both look at the ass whipping taking place. He shrugs, reaches out for me, figures he should get in the son-beating business. So I did what any kid would have done—

SWAINO   BAM! Like a streak of midget lightning, he bolts like a bitch out the front door.

FRANK   Except the screen door was fucking locked.

SWAINO   He smashes right through it, keeps running. Everybody just stops for a second and we all look out across the lawn.

FRANK   And there's little Packie running down the middle of the street with a fucking screen door hanging around his neck.

SWAINO   Me and Frank, we used the diversion to escape.

PACKIE   We all met in the woods by this big rock where we'd go.

SWAINO   Just a big fucking rock in the woods. That's all it took back then.

PACKIE   I snuck over a bottle I had swiped from my dad's car.

SWAINO   First time any of us had Scotch.

PACKIE   It tasted like shit, didn't it?

FRANK*'s cell rings. He looks at the number.*

FRANK   I gotta take this. Chad, you in a rush?

CHAD   I can hang for a few.

FRANK   Be right back, bro. (*Into cell phone.*) This is Frank Romanowski. Just gimme one minute, please.

FRANK *walks out.*

SWAINO   Season tickets, huh? You must be fucking rolling in it.

CHAD   My dad does pretty good.

PACKIE   What's he do?

CHAD   He's a partner at Nutter, McClennen and Fish. It's a law firm in Boston.

SWAINO   What's that like? Having a father you're not ashamed of?

CHAD   Good, I guess.

PACKIE   He ever need, like, a driver or something?

SWAINO   Give it a rest, Packie.

PACKIE   I know Boston like the back of my hand.

SWAINO   Nobody wants your midget ass driving them around Boston. So be honest. Frank sucks at hoops, right?

CHAD   He's pretty good. Takes it very seriously.

PACKIE   He's always been very competitive.

SWAINO   I wanna know about Northeastern pussy. Is it good?

CHAD   Yeah.

SWAINO   Yeah! I thought so! Just, like, go on.

CHAD   Well, you know, being on the team plus in a fraternity definitely helps.

PACKIE   You're a good looking guy too. Don't discount that.

CHAD   So, yeah, I had a great freshman year for the most part.

SWAINO   Goddammit, I remember my freshman year. Fucking insane. My advice? Don't commit, kid. Just keep trying the flavors. Last thing you want is some girl tying you down.

PACKIE   What if he meets the right girl?

SWAINO   What is this, *Sex and the City*? Shut the fuck up. Girls, most of them, they can be a lot of trouble.

CHAD   Tell me about it.

SWAINO You gotta be careful. Especially when you're an athlete like us.

CHAD You played ball at Keene State?

SWAINO I meant high school. You gotta be careful with girls. They try to trap you. Happened to me all the time.

PACKIE What do you mean "trap you?"

SWAINO It never happened to you so you wouldn't understand.

PACKIE I call bullshit.

CHAD No, he's right. They do.

SWAINO See? He knows exactly what I mean. Don't you, kid?

CHAD I actually . . . there was an incident I went through recently.

SWAINO Yeah?

CHAD This girl kept showing up at our parties on the weekends, I didn't really know her but she was pretty hot so we hooked up a few times.

SWAINO And?

CHAD Well it snowballed into this whole controversy.

PACKIE What kind of controversy?

CHAD She started texting me naked pictures.

SWAINO I like where this is headed.

CHAD I showed a couple friends in my fraternity because . . . I was always saying that one of her nipples was shaped like Florida and they didn't believe me.

SWAINO You needed their opinion.

CHAD Right, just like you are with your buddies, you know? It became a thing in the house so I had the girl send me more pictures and started texting them around to settle the argument and then it got kinda out of control. Pretty soon these pics were being sent all over campus.

PACKIE We call that "going viral."

SWAINO Thanks for the clarification, professor cuntface.

CHAD Then the girl showed up to a party and everyone started calling her "Panhandle."

SWAINO Settles the debate, at least.

CHAD Girl ran off, like, devastated.

SWAINO College girls, everything's the end of the world.

CHAD Ends up she didn't go to Northeastern, she was still in high school. One of my fraternity brothers had sent the pics to his cousin who went to the same school as she did. He put them online, ended up on front page of Reddit. Within three days everybody at her high school was calling her "Panhandle." And, uh . . . she took a bunch of pills and tried to kill herself.

SWAINO Jesus.

CHAD I know. Crazy, right?

PACKIE Is she okay now?

CHAD I don't know. She was, like, in a coma for a while, I know that. My dad is, you know, a lawyer and he told me not to get involved. He's really connected, kept it out of the news. I'm trying not to focus on it.

SWAINO The cops didn't get involved?

CHAD My dad made sure that no charges were filed. Ten years from now, I don't want some misunderstanding blowing my chances at becoming a partner, you know? It's like, Northeastern, they threatened to take me off the team because of it. My dad fucked them up too. They can't do that kind of shit.

PACKIE That's a tragic story, Chad.

CHAD I felt really bad but . . . honestly, like my dad said, she shouldn't have sent the pictures to begin with.

SWAINO Look, maybe we should talk about something else . . .

FRANK *comes back in.*

FRANK What's going on?

SWAINO We're just shooting the shit with the kid.

FRANK Yeah? About what?

PACKIE Talking about pussy, you know.

PACKIE *hops up on the counter—misses and crashes to the floor.*

FRANK So why is everyone so quiet alla sudden?

PACKIE Frank, it's nothing.

FRANK Chad, what were you talking about?

CHAD Girls.

FRANK Okay, so why can't I be told that?

SWAINO Frank, relax.

FRANK I'm just fucking curious.

PACKIE Well Chad here was recollecting about what it's like to be an athlete, how a lot of romantic opportunities arise.

FRANK Romantic opportunities?

CHAD I think I'm gonna go.

FRANK Before you go, Chad. Just fill me in.

SWAINO Why you gotta make a fucking big deal about everything?

FRANK I don't like secrets. Especially when it's in my place, with my fucking booze. Okay? Tell me what you were talking about.

CHAD Nothing.

FRANK Weird everyone would act so fucking strange over nothing. Tell me what you were fucking saying!

CHAD Packie?

PACKIE Swaino had drinks with Karen!

SWAINO Packie, you moron!

FRANK My Karen?

SWAINO She Facebooked me.

FRANK And?

SWAINO And we had a drink.

FRANK Did you fuck her?

SWAINO What? No, of course not! I would never do that to you!

FRANK So why did you meet?

PACKIE   Calm down, Frank.

FRANK   Stay out of this, Packie! Why did you meet Karen for drinks?

SWAINO   She was worried about your daughter. Yeah, that's right. Frank has a daughter. Cat's outta the bag. Still think he's cool?

FRANK   And she called you?

SWAINO   She Facebooked me. Said she couldn't get any of you guys to call her back. She wanted to know your new address and was about to follow you home from work. I said we could meet. I was protecting you.

FRANK   So you did this behind my back?

SWAINO   What did you want me to do?

FRANK   Fucking call me first!

SWAINO   And have you act like this! It's not my fault Crystal won't call her fucking mother back!

CHAD *runs for the door but can't open it due to the tricky lock. In a flash,* FRANK *pulls a heavy crescent wrench off the tool wall, crosses the room and CRACKS* CHAD *over the head.* CHAD *falls to the floor in a heap.* FRANK *tosses the wrench noisily aside.*

PACKIE   You just hit Chad Walker on the head with a wrench.

SWAINO   What the fuck you do that for, Frank?

PACKIE   Frank?

FRANK *takes a shot of Johnny.*

FRANK   That thing he was telling you about. It's Crystal.

PACKIE   Holy shit, what a coincidence.

SWAINO   It's not a coincidence, you fucking retard.

PACKIE   So the one who took the pills is Crystal? Jesus Christ! Are you sure?

SWAINO   What the fuck are doing, Frank?

FRANK   What does it look like I'm doing?

FRANK *pulls out a gun and duct tape.*

PACKIE   Jesus Christ! Are you going to rape him?

FRANK   What?

SWAINO   What's a matter with you?

PACKIE   I'm high and I'm drunk and I'm very easily confused!

Over the following exchanges, FRANK *prepares for the task by producing the duffel bag he stashed at the top of show and begins removing CORPSE BREAKDOWN AND DISPOSAL TOOLS onto the countertop:*

- *Rubber gloves*

- *Smocks*

- *Heavy duty plastic bags*

- *Cotton towels*

- *Plastic tarps*

- *Plastic bucket*

- *Scrub brush*

- *Hammer, chisel*

Rogue Machine Theatre   Photo: John P. Flynn

- *Massive cleaver*

- *Hacksaw, handsaw, pruning shears*

- *Splash visor*

SWAINO He's got a gun, Packie. Use your fucking head.

PACKIE He's gonna kill Chad Walker?

SWAINO Seems like it.

PACKIE Right in front of us?

SWAINO I'm assuming he wants our help.

PACKIE Is this really happening?

FRANK All the shit we've been through together? I thought we were a fucking team here!

SWAINO A team? This is your plan?

FRANK Whenever you guys have needed me, I've been there. Every fucking time.

FRANK *pulls* CHAD *onto the chair and duct-tapes his arms to it.*

PACKIE You never killed anybody for us, Frank! Changed my pants maybe, loaned me some money. But definitely no killing.

FRANK I can't do this by myself. I'll pull the trigger, but I need you guys here with me. And there's a lot of work with disposal.

PACKIE Disposal?

SWAINO Jesus Fucking Christ! I coulda been anywhere tonight . . .

PACKIE This is why he called us?

SWAINO Yeah, this is WAY better than strippers!

FRANK *opens a tarp and lays it out on the floor. He places a chair in the center.*

PACKIE   Where'd you get the gun, Frank?

FRANK   Seriously? Out of all the shit going on right now you ask me where I got the gun?

PACKIE   Because if you shoot him, they'll know.

FRANK   They won't know.

SWAINO   You have a plan?

FRANK *reaches into his bag and pulls out a three page printout with graphic diagrams and photos.*

FRANK   I downloaded instructions off the internet. Here's how to dismember, debone, and deflesh a two hundred pound corpse in an hour. Here's how you break down bone, skin and muscle with chemicals. I got those out back. And here's how you get rid of the slurry and clean up. Fucking internet.

SWAINO   Does Karen know what happened to Crystal?

PACKIE   Not sure you should bring her up her right now!

FRANK   Last thing Crystal needs right now is that train wreck.

SWAINO   She's still the mother. She should know what's going on.

PACKIE   With the Chad Walker situation?

SWAINO   No, with the Crystal situation.

FRANK   Why are you fucking with me right now?

SWAINO   I'm trying to help you, Frank.

FRANK You both heard what happened to Crystal and you know what? Neither of you motherfuckers have even asked how she is!

FRANK lifts CHAD's unconscious body and plops him in the chair.

PACKIE You're right, Frank. Sorry.

SWAINO How is she?

FRANK Two weeks ago she overdosed. Messed with her nervous system. She went into respiratory arrest, threw her into a coma for six days. We don't know the extent of the damage. She can talk a little now . . .

SWAINO Jesus Christ.

FRANK Only time's gonna tell . . . even with insurance, I'm running out of money . . . do you understand what he did to her?

FRANK begins duct-taping CHAD's arms and legs to the chair.

SWAINO Frank, I know you're upset but let's talk about this first.

FRANK You wanna talk?

SWAINO Not really, to be honest.

FRANK You see now, Swaino? You see what your behavior does?

SWAINO Me?

FRANK Yes you! I've been warning you about this for twenty fucking years!

SWAINO What the fuck did I do?

MCC/Lortel   Photo: Joan Marcus

FRANK You create this hostile environment for women to get treated like meat.

SWAINO I never did anything remotely like this Chad Walker bullshit!

FRANK You contribute to a world that lets this shit happen.

SWAINO I got six sisters, man. Deep down, you know I respect women.

PACKIE This ain't Swaino's fault.

FRANK And you. All that fucking porn on the internet you look at. Those girls have lives and feelings and fathers that worry about them. You ever stop and think about that?

PACKIE I worship women. They just kinda scare me is all.

SWAINO This ain't our fault, Frank.

FRANK Until you knew he was talking about Crystal, you guys fucking *laughed* at the girl in that story. That tells me everything I gotta know.

PACKIE I'm sorry, Frank.

FRANK For what?

PACKIE A variety of things. That's why I'm gonna help.

PACKIE *finds a full-body hazmat suit in the bag and starts putting it on. He also finds a protective visor, puts that on too.*

PACKIE To catch the splash damage . . . good thinking!

SWAINO Have you done this before, Packie?

PACKIE Fuck no. But I watch a shitload of *CSI*.

FRANK   Swaino, if you wanna go, you can go.

SWAINO   I've been trying to go all night!

FRANK   Well go!

SWAINO   I'm already a fucking accessory!

PACKIE   Nobody's gonna find out!

SWAINO   This ain't a fucking TV show, idiot! In real life people get caught.

PACKIE   It's the opposite.

SWAINO   What?

PACKIE   In TV, they got an hour to solve a case, nobody'd watch it if there wasn't closure every night. Just because the public demands resolution don't mean it's realistic. It's wish fulfillment. Like the Rocky franchise. You really think a short Italian could beat up a massively muscular black guy in real life—

SWAINO   It just seems like Frank didn't plan this out very fucking well!

FRANK   Sure I did!

SWAINO   You talked to him on your cell phone, right?

FRANK   It's a burner!

SWAINO   What the fuck's a "burner?"

PACKIE   Don't you watch *The Wire*?

SWAINO   What? Listen, kid's fucking nineteen, people are gonna wonder where he is.

FRANK   He's a drug dealer.

SWAINO He's a very casual drug dealer.

FRANK Are you defending him?

SWAINO I'm just pointing out that he's not fucking Scarface here.

PACKIE You heard what he did to Crystal? He fucking deserves this!

SWAINO Yes, I know. But this whole fucking . . . ok, remember earlier where I was saying your temper sometimes gets you into trouble?

FRANK Yeah?

SWAINO You see how it's being illustrated here!

CHAD *wakes up.* FRANK *gets the gun.*

PACKIE Guys, Chad Walker's awake!

CHAD Please . . . don't do this . . .

FRANK Your ass ain't getting away with this shit, Chad.

CHAD Swaino, help me.

SWAINO Don't get me involved, kid.

CHAD Wait! Stop! Let me just say something. Please.

FRANK What?

CHAD I'm sorry.

SWAINO That's your response? "Sorry?"

PACKIE I thought this prick went to college?

CHAD I'm just a kid. Please! I made a mistake. My parents . . . it's just . . . the internet and . . . I'm sorry. I know I hurt her, I didn't mean it.

FRANK I was younger than you when she was born, you know that? Seventeen years we've been together. Making it work. A lot of sacrifices. A lot of compromises. But I wasn't alone. Back in the day, my friends here were more of a family to Crystal than her own mother. Me, I worked in this shop every day for fifteen fucking years to give her a future. But now, instead of filling out college packets, she's laying in a hospital bed on a respirator. All because you came along and you treated her like a piece of garbage. Was it funny passing around that picture of my baby girl? Bet you all got a big fucking laugh, right?

CHAD Jesus Christ, you can't shoot me over this.

FRANK Which part? Ruining her life or ruining mine?

CHAD I have $112,000 in my savings account!

SWAINO Oh, fuck.

FRANK Cover his face.

CHAD I'm sorry. Frank, I'm sorry!

FRANK *tosses* PACKIE *a pillow case.*

CHAD Please . . . please . . . PLEASE! My mom and dad! Let me say goodbye to them . . . please . . .

PACKIE *holds up the tarp to catch the splash damage behind* CHAD.

PACKIE Swaino, grab the other end.

SWAINO Oh, man. Oh, man . . . this is bad . . .

MCC/Lortel   Photo: Joan Marcus

SWAINO *reluctantly takes the other end of the tarp and they hold it up.* CHAD *hyperventilates as* FRANK *puts the gun up to* CHAD*'s head (screaming NO! over and over again). The whole room tenses as* FRANK *is about to pull the trigger . . .*

PACKIE *SCREAMS!*

PACKIE Foursquare!

FRANK What?

PACKIE He checked in! (*Beat . . . they don't get it.*) He Foursquared. We all did.

SWAINO Put down the gun, Frank!

FRANK What's Foursquare again?

SWAINO Fucking asshole posted on his Facebook that he was here.

CHAD I have two thousand eight hundred and fifty-four friends!

PACKIE You have two thousand eight hundred and fifty-four friends?

FRANK Somebody fucking explain!

SWAINO It's a fucking internet thing. All a cop has to do is look on his Facebook and see he was here tonight. See all of us were. It's a big fucking bullseye right on our backs.

PACKIE Swaino's right.

FRANK *lowers the gun.*

CHAD This is unbelievable.

SWAINO Shut the fuck up!

CHAD I'll tell you what you're gonna do, guys. You're gonna untie me and I'm gonna call the cops. Attempted murder, kidnapping, assault!

SWAINO Shut up!

CHAD My father is gonna sue the shit out of you! You guys are gonna get ass raped in jail! Get ready! Start stretching those asses, boys!

PACKIE Shut the fuck up!

CHAD You wanna talk accountability? Let's talk accountability, Frank. Tell your daughter to stop texting naked pictures of herself!

FRANK *seizes* CHAD*'s neck with his hands, starts strangling him.*

PACKIE You gotta stop, Frank.

PACKIE *tries to stop him.* FRANK *is too strong for him.* CHAD *is gagging, dying under that pillowcase.*

SWAINO Frank, stop!

SWAINO *joins in, is able to pry* FRANK *off* CHAD. *As* CHAD *gasps for breath:*

FRANK Why did she send those pictures?

PACKIE It's fucking technology, man. Never before in history has this much shit been possible. Nobody knows how to handle it yet.

FRANK But I don't understand why she sent them.

SWAINO She just wanted him to like her.

CHAD (*Voice raw.*) You're going to jail, big guy. She's gonna miss you!

PACKIE Maybe you should skip town, Frank.

FRANK What if she needs me?

SWAINO You stay they'll lock you up. Especially after the window incident.

FRANK But she'll know where I am.

PACKIE Maybe you can plead insanity.

CHAD Are you kidding me? This is fucking pre-meditated! You did some serious shopping here. My father is so fucking good at what he does it's scary. See, he went to college. He made something of himself. People like you don't win.

SWAINO SHUT THE FUCK UP!

Now it's SWAINO*'s turn to beat* CHAD *with a massive right cross.* FRANK *pulls him off with great effort, slaps him across the face to get him stop.*

FRANK Terence, calm down! There's nothing else you can do. I'll cop a plea to get you guys off, say you had nothing to do with this. Which is the truth. I coerced you into coming here. You guys are all I got . . . I'm fucking sorry.

SWAINO It's okay, Frank.

FRANK Give me a half hour head start before you let him go. I need to see her before I turn myself in.

PACKIE Okay.

FRANK Keep an eye on her, guys. You gotta do better than I did.

FRANK *walks toward the door.*

CHAD So sad. One bad decision can change your whole god-damn life.

SWAINO Frank!

FRANK What?

SWAINO I got an idea.

FRANK What?

SWAINO Packie, does my phone have a camera?

PACKIE Of course.

FRANK Why?

SWAINO One photo can ruin a life, right?

FRANK What kind of a photo we talking about?

SWAINO Packie, you wanna make sure Frank doesn't go to jail?

PACKIE More than anything.

SWAINO Pull out your cock. We're taking some pictures.

PACKIE Why mine?

SWAINO For one, it's by far the most photogenic. And two . . . your fault with this fucking FOURSQUARE BULLSHIT!

PACKIE This is the plan?

SWAINO Can you think of another option?

PACKIE *thinks about it for a good five seconds.*

PACKIE No.

He starts taking off the smock.

CHAD   What's going on?

SWAINO   I'm gonna need you to shut the fuck up.

CHAD   This is only going to get worse for you.

SWAINO   We got nothing to lose.

Like any good photographer, SWAINO *holds out his hands to "frame" the image and begins "preparing" the scene for the ultimate photograph. He grabs a box, places it beside* CHAD.

SWAINO   Packie, get up there.

PACKIE *gets on the box, practices a few poses with his pelvis jutting out as* SWAINO *frames up.*

SWAINO   Guys, kill the fucking lights.

As PACKIE *gets on the stool (his back to the audience),* FRANK *hits the light switch, the set goes almost dark.* SWAINO *finds a powerful flashlight, positions it. He frames it again . . . still unsatisfied, he opens the refrigerator door and gets the exact visual he wants.*

SWAINO   Do it, Packie.

PACKIE *stands on it so he has one foot on the stool, one on the back of* CHAD*'s chair and his crotch hovers above* CHAD*'s face. He is about to pull his penis out but hesitates.* SWAINO, *seeing* PACKIE *hesitate, grabs the bottle of Johnny Walker Blue and hands it to him.*

SWAINO   You can do this, Packie.

PACKIE I don't know, guys. This just seems a little gay.

SWAINO I think that's the fucking point, Pack.

PACKIE *takes a monster slug of whisky. He hands the whisky bottle back, then unzips his pants as his massive penis drops down into view, silhouetted by the flashlight and fridge light. It dangles there . . . a good ten inches long.*

SWAINO Take it off.

PACKIE *starts pulling off his shirt . . .*

SWAINO Not your shirt! The fucking hood!

PACKIE *pulls the pillowcase off.* CHAD *is staring at a penis in his face.*

CHAD What the fuck is this?

SWAINO Put it in your mouth.

CHAD No way.

SWAINO Okay. Hey, Frank.

SWAINO *hands* FRANK *the gun.* FRANK *jams the gun up against* CHAD*'s face.*

FRANK Open your mouth.

CHAD No way!

FRANK *jams the gun in* CHAD*'s crotch.*

FRANK Open your mouth or I'll shoot your fucking dick off! I don't care if I'm going to jail, do you understand!

Petrified, CHAD *opens his mouth.*

SWAINO Do it, Packie!

PACKIE *jams his penis in* CHAD*'s open mouth.* SWAINO *holds up his camera phone.* CHAD *is gagging,* PACKIE *is gagging.*

PACKIE Hurry up!

SWAINO It says it's "loading!"

PACKIE Just press the button on the top!

SWAINO Sorry, it's going to a different fucking screen!

PACKIE Press the button!

SWAINO Frank, the gun is in the frame.

FRANK Sorry.

PACKIE TAKE THE FUCKING PICTURE!

SWAINO Okay, I got it! I got it!

PACKIE *jumps off and puts his dick away.* CHAD *pukes.* SWAINO *shows* FRANK *the picture.*

FRANK Show him.

PACKIE Can you tell that it's me?

SWAINO Only if somebody has seen your cock. So I think you're safe.

SWAINO *shows* CHAD *the picture.*

SWAINO Really captured your eyes in this one. Okay Chad, I'm gonna explain the situation because you look a little confused as to what just transpired here. Totally understandable. You just had a huge cock jammed down your throat, that's gotta be traumatic. Option one, we let you go and you run to your pop and cry like a fucking bitch and you sic the cops on our asses. But before the cops find us, my little friend here, he's a social networking fucking genius. He's gonna post this cute little photo all over the internet. Like the entire thing. It'll do that thing . . . what the fuck is it called?

PACKIE   Going viral.

SWAINO   It'll go fucking viral! And once everybody hears the story behind it. Every basketball player, frat brother, chicks on campus, even Nutter, Macallan and whateverthefuck. Your dad works there, right? Everybody will see it. Who knows, maybe they'll even come up with a little cute nickname for ya.

PACKIE   Yeah! Like "Captain Dick Sucker!"

SWAINO   Well, hopefully they'll be more creative than that, but yes, something along those lines. You wanna hear option two, Chad? Option two, you walk out of here and never speak of tonight to anyone, anywhere, ever. It'll be like this whole night . . . including this photo . . . never fucking happened. Which one you going with, Chad?

CHAD   Option two.

SWAINO   Good boy.

SWAINO *hands* PACKIE *a utility knife, which he uses to slash the duct tape and free* CHAD. CHAD *gets up and* FRANK, *gun in hand, takes a few menacing steps toward him. After a moment,* FRANK *puts the gun on the counter.*

FRANK   Get the fuck outta my shop.

CHAD *walks out . . . as he leaves:*

PACKIE   You don't fuck with Manch-Vegas!

FRANK *virtually collapses, spent. He catches the sign . . . his eyes linger on the photo of a young Crystal.*

SWAINO   She's gonna be okay.

After a moment, FRANK *talks:*

FRANK   When she was little, she got upset, it was easier. I'd just hold her. Give her attention. I was everything she needed. It just gets so fucking complicated out there.

PACKIE   You're the best father I've ever seen, Frank. Even though that might not be saying much considering where we all came from.

SWAINO   She's gonna be okay.

FRANK   I don't know . . .

PACKIE   The way they are with technology these days, they can do wonders.

FRANK   All those years, resenting my life . . . I think she sensed that. I think I made her feel like a piece of shit.

SWAINO   No, man. You gotta put out positive thoughts.

PACKIE   Positive thoughts.

SWAINO   Say it. Say "She's gonna be okay."

PACKIE   She's gonna be—

SWAINO Not you, idiot.

PACKIE Sorry.

SWAINO Bottom line. We should have been there for you and Crystal.

PACKIE We let you guys down.

SWAINO I promise you, that's not gonna happen ever again. Okay?

PACKIE Okay?

FRANK *grips* SWAINO *with his hand as* PACKIE *absentmindedly strokes* FRANK*'s knee.* FRANK *and* SWAINO *shoot* PACKIE *a look.*

PACKIE Sorry.

PACKIE *lifts his hand off and* FRANK *reaches out for him, holding his two best friends as the lights fade to black and Crystal's sign stares over them.*

THE END.